Enjoying Life Again

Petra Schürmann and Dr. med. Gerhard Freund report on how they got over the worst crisis in their lives with the nutritive substance NADH

Publisher: Gesundheitsprodukte Kornelia Sinning

Authors: Schürmann, Petra / Freund, Dr. Gerhard

Enjoying Life Again

Published by BOD-Verlag, November 2016

English translation: Marianne Littlewood

German edition published by BOD-Verlag, October 2010

Wieder Freude am Leben. Geheimnis der Lebensenergie – Gesundheit der Zellen.

Production and Publishing House:

BoD - Books on Demand, Norderstedt

www.bod.de

Enjoying Life Again

ISBN: 978-3-7431-4659-4

Notice:

Medicine as a science is subject to continuous development. Research as well as experience widen our insight, particularly with respect to required levels of nutrients and the application of nutritional supplements. The reader may well trust the authors and the publisher to have spared no effort in making statements, concerning the required levels and dosages, the possible applications of nutritional supplements or pharmaceutical products mentioned in this book, in accordance with the current level of knowledge at the time the book was completed. Nevertheless, the user or reader is requested to check carefully the instructions enclosed with the products mentioned to find out whether the indications and recommendations mentioned therein are different from the statements made in this book. Where necessary, the practitioner (physician or alternative practitioner) should be consulted. Protected trademarks may not have been specifically identified in all cases. However, in case there is no such indication, this does not necessarily imply that it is not a trademarked name.

All rights reserved, Copyright:

Gesundheitsprodukte Kornelia Sinning
Max-Hufschmidt-Str. 4, 55130 Mainz, Germany
Kornelia.Sinning@t-online.de

This book describes the importance of NADH (nicotinamide adenine dinucleotide hydride), otherwise known as Co-Enzyme 1, for our wellbeing and health.

NADH is the only substance which, as of yet, has been scientifically proven to raise the level of energy in our cells.

NADH extends the lifetime of our cells and can prevent deficiencies and illness in the body.

The effects of NADH were demonstrated by the Austrian scientist Prof. Dr. Dr. Georg Birkmayer in many years of research.

The more NADH the body has available, the more powerful and vital we will feel.

NADH is a natural anti-ageing agent that makes you both feel and look younger.

NADH is recommended by an increasing number of doctors, alternative practitioners and beauticians.

Find out more about the nutritive substance NADH, how it was discovered and how it can help to fight disease and premature ageing.

"It is not only sick people who benefit from this all-round remedy from the world of dietary supplements, everybody can", says Dr. Freund.

This book will tell you how.

"To invest money in NADH is like a health insurance which could well make extensive, medical treatment totally unnecessary", writes Dr. Freund.

NADH is highly acclaimed by celebrities and top athletes.

Table of Contents

The Hippocratic Oath	9
My poor Gerhard	11
My poor Petra	15
How I discovered NADH for us	21
Experiences of a befriended doctor	25
Everybody wants to get old – but nobody wants to be old!	28
NADH – The anti-ageing enzyme	32
How to stay younger thanks to NADH – and have a longer life	34
Who needs NADH?	37
What is an antioxidant?	41
What is NADH?	47
What is the actual effect of NADH?	50
NADH repairs damaged DNA	54
NADH helps patients with Chronic Fatigue Syndrome	56
NADH and Parkinson's disease	59
NADH and Alzheimer's disease	62
NADH against depression	64

NADH and performance …………..……..	66
NADH and the memory ……………..............	69
NADH against ageing and disease …………	71
Summary …………………………....…......	73
Sources / Bibliography ………….....……….	75
In which cases could NADH be helpful? …..	78

The Hippocratic Oath

"I swear by Apollo the physician, and Aesculapius the surgeon, likewise Hygeia and Panacea, and call all the gods and goddesses to witness, that I will observe and keep this underwritten oath, to the utmost of my power and judgment. I will reverence my master who taught me the art; equally with my parents, will I allow him things necessary for his support, and will consider his sons as brothers. I will teach them my art without reward or agreement; and I will impart all my acquirement, instructions, and whatever I know, to my master's children, as to my own; and likewise to all my pupils, who shall bind and tie themselves by a professional oath, but to none else. With regard to healing the sick, I will devise and order for them the best diet, according to my judgment and means; and I will take care that they suffer no hurt or damage. Nor shall any man's entreaty prevail upon me to administer poison to anyone; neither will I counsel any man to do so. Moreover, I will give no sort of medicine to any pregnant woman, with a view to destroy the child. Further, I will comport myself and use my knowledge in a godly manner. I will not cut for the stone, but will commit that affair entirely to the surgeons. Whatsoever house I may enter, my visit shall be for the convenience and advantage of the patient. And I will willingly refrain from doing any injury or wrong from falsehood, and (in an especial manner) from acts of an amorous nature, whatever may be the rank of those who it may be my duty to cure, whether mistress or servant, bond or free. Whatever, in the course of my practice, I may see or hear (even when not invited), whatever I may happen to obtain knowledge of, if it be not

proper to repeat it, I will keep sacred and secret within my own breast. If I faithfully observe this oath, may I thrive and prosper in my fortune and profession, and live in the estimation of posterity; or on breach thereof, may the reverse be my fate!"

Dear Reader,

I swore the Hippocratic Oath, in the same way as my father and my grandfather did before me. The Freunds are a family with 169 years of experience in the field of medicine. I usually say that we have that neurotic need to help contained in our genes and therefore cannot do any other job but that of a doctor.

As a physician, you want to help and you must help. But time and time again, there are situations where you are not in a position to help and therefore feel totally helpless.

My wife Petra and I experienced that kind of situation on 21 June 2001. On that day, we lost our daughter Alexandra who was killed by a wrong-way driver on the motorway between Munich and Salzburg.

During the time that followed, we received consolation and support in the form of letters, cards and recordings from more than 8,000 people. This helped us 8,000 times, and it encouraged us 8,000 times. We read every single line and thereby experienced that our fate was neither unique nor particularly hard or particularly mean. In view of the grief of other fathers and mothers mourning the death of their child, our fate became fate no. 8001 – which made it more tangible and understandable to us.

I was not able to help my daughter on her fateful day. And, up until the summer of 2003, it seemed that I was not able to help my wife with her grief and pain. However, fortunately I then heard about the nutritional substance NADH. With this discovery, joy came back to our lives. First to me, and then to my wife also.

On the following pages, Petra and I will try to describe how we successfully got over the worst crisis in our lives. We hope that we will be able to help those who need help, or are searching for it. Surely, there are many of them. Day after day in this country alone, hundreds, if not thousands of people lose a loved one and, because of that, are hit by a deep mental and physical crisis.

Dr. Gerhard Freund

My poor Gerhard

We want to describe how we found joy in life again – and how our life has changed since we started taking the nutritive substance NADH in the summer of 2003. In order to understand what has become so much better, so much easier and so much more positive in our lives, however, you have to know how it all started. I will try to illustrate as objectively as possible the condition in which my husband was after Alexandra passed away. In the next chapter, Gerhard will then try to describe my mental, emotional and physical condition before we discovered NADH.

Petra Schürmann:

Only a few weeks before my only daughter Alexandra was born, my mother had died. Several years ago, my father passed away. The day of Alexandra's passing on 21 June 2001 was, therefore, not the first time I and my family had encountered death. However, the loss of my father and mother could not in any way prepare me for the loss of my daughter.

Grief, to me, is a feeling of saying good-bye, of letting go. Love, to me, is a feeling of existence and touching. Now that more than two years have passed after her death, I do not love her any less than on any day of her life.

Whenever I think of Alexandra – which I am doing continuously - I sense a great, deep love, but at the same time, a roaring, painful feeling of homesickness. I miss her body, I miss her smell, I miss the sound of her voice. My longing for her is overwhelming. The pain is just as hard as it was on the very first day. I have had to learn the bitter lesson that time does not heal any wounds – even though I have managed to participate in life again and feel physically and emotionally balanced.

My husband Gerhard also loved Alexandra. However, unlike me – he let her go. I think that this way of grieving was easier for him because it is more usual and better accepted by the outside world. Maybe letting go of her was his decision because he is a man and because men react in a more rational way than women when faced with an extreme situation.

Gerhard was devastated by Alexandra's death. Shortly after the funeral, I had seriously feared for his life. When he got a normal flu jab, he had experienced a strong allergic reaction that completely shattered him, in a situation where he had already been mentally and physically troubled. What troubled me most, however, was not so much that the grief had obviously lowered the level of his immune system dramatically and that he had become sick after a harmless vaccination; what was even worse was that the doctor inside of him had totally failed.

Gerhard did not fight, he gave in. He smoked like a chimney. He would not step into a car. He withdrew not only from me, from neighbours and friends, but from life altogether. Sometimes he woke up screaming during the night and I had to comfort him.

I was no longer able to recognize my husband. Despite having worked as a senior physician for cancer specialist Dr. Josef Issels in Rottach-Egern and having been faced with so much pain and death, he was now not able to come to terms with his own pain. Instead of strengthening his immune system, as he had recommended to other bereaved persons over and over again, he had mentally and physically ruined himself.

I was not able to support him during that extremely critical time. Besides, I was too preoccupied with myself. There did not seem to be a common bridge that might join us together in our pain. Gerhard used to say that he was communicating with Alexandra. Yet he was unable to talk to me about either that communication, or about Alexandra.

We took very different paths after our daughter died. We mourned in completely different ways and we coped in different ways. I wanted to communicate my pain to the outside world while Gerhard fell silent. I would go to Alexandra's grave almost every day. Gerhard has only been there a few times since the funeral took place. For a long time, we were not well and our partnership was at stake because we were totally exhausted, both physically and mentally, and could not therefore find the strength to support and comfort our partner during the most difficult time of our lives.

Today, things are different. Gerhard, just like me, is enjoying life again. We are able to talk to each other again. We can set new common goals. Ever since Gerhard has been taking his NADH pill in the morning, he feels more strength inside, he thinks positively and has completely opened up to life again. He has become a different person, somehow younger and more open. He is back again. Since 2003, there has not been a single summer's day when he did not get up at five in the morning to do his laps in the pool. It is even possible to talk about a holiday trip. I notice that Gerhard wants to live again, that he wants to get something out of life.

Some time ago, he even left the house together with me, he got into my car and we accepted an invitation. Both the Munich society and the press were totally surprised to see him wearing a tuxedo and me wearing an evening dress when we appeared at a public event at Schleißheim castle. He quite enjoyed being among other people, making small talk about politics, the economy and other things.

The grief is not yet over. However, thanks to NADH, with Gerhard's new physical and mental energy, life and joy have come back to us. That is what I am grateful for.

My poor Petra

The famous Ringberg Hospital in Rottach-Egern, Bavaria, run by Dr. Issels, only admitted cancer patients who had been given up on by at least two doctors beforehand. Survival was seen as a miracle there and death was an everyday routine. I was a senior physician in that cancer clinic for more than 10 years. For many patients, it was a hospice. I have certainly seen a lot of suffering. Yet nothing could compare with what I saw in the face and eyes of my wife.

What my wife Petra actually went through after our daughter Alexandra's death is hard to express and even harder to describe. There was nothing theatrical or spectacular. Petra did not collapse. Petra did not burst out crying or screaming. Petra did not complain. Petra did not grumble. Outwardly, she appeared as calm and unperturbed as usual. If there had not been this tremendous loss of weight after a few months that made her beautiful face look so lean, outsiders would hardly have noticed any change in her. I have known Petra for almost 40 years now. When I look at her, I know how she feels.

We live at Lake Starnberg, pretty close to the mountains. Those who like the alpine regions will know that the weather conditions there can get really critical – sometimes within a few seconds. During a period of changeable weather in the Alps, one might look one way and see a clear, blue sky with sunshine. However, if you turn the other way, the sky might be frightening, with a threatening, black colour and there may sometimes even be darting flashes of lightning. An experienced mountain lover will immediately realize that serious danger is ahead.

Likewise, Petra was in an explosive state of change after Alexandra's funeral. As I have said, this went unnoticed from the outside. However, inside of her, she grew darker and darker every day, more and more desperate and perilous. For a long time, I was not able to judge which of the two moods would prevail. For months, I feared that the dark side would win. Petra thought about suicide a thousand times. I spent these months clearing the house of any hard drugs that might have had a deadly effect if used in a high dose.

Petra usually starts the day at 8 o'clock and finishes late at night. She looks after the house and the big garden. She does the cooking and cleaning, she is also writing a book – her fifth! She uses the car to go shopping twice a week. This is what she has always done, even on a day when she may not actually feel strong enough to do it. Petra is enormously disciplined. I have never seen her hanging around. She goes about her daily work like a precision clock, always precise, always punctual. In a recent interview, she confided to the reporter: "Having grown up with a downright protestant ethic and self-discipline, I cannot do anything about that. The feeling of hanging around is so unfamiliar to me that I can't even imagine how to do it."

When Alexandra died, we were at the top of the media's interest, and most organs reacted reasonably and treated us quite fairly. One magazine, however, reported that on one of her visits to our daughter's grave, Petra did not wear any make-up. This detail was obviously supposed to give the reader the impression that Petra Schürmann was already run-down physically and emotionally, to the point where she was not able to put on any make-up. This lie was a huge insult to Petra. Lies and slander usually hit Petra very hard, much more than her own suffering.

When the news of Alexandra's death arrived, it left Petra virtually speechless. She was still able to speak, but not with the same vigour and fluency as before. She had, and still has, to struggle with every sentence. Every word she wants to utter demands all of her energy. Thanks to NADH, which I have given to her since the summer of 2003, this is getting better as well, although at a very, very slow pace.

Petra's speech disorder was clearly due to a psychological blockage. As a doctor, I could see that immediately. Of course, I had a solution to her problem.

I asked my wife to undergo a logopaedic treatment. For non-professionals: Speech therapy is a medical field that deals with speech and hearing impairments, as well as with stammering. Petra went to see a speech therapist. She also went to a psychiatrist. Neither treatment showed any results at all.

I have already said that I have never seen as much pain as I saw in Petra's face and eyes. I have said that following Alexandra's death, Petra not only lived in a particularly dark and painful world, but every attempt to free her from this prison of grief and suffering failed miserably after a short time.

Petra is my wife. For me, as the doctor in the family, she was both a patient and a case during those months of massive crisis. And, I have to say that for a long time she was a hopeless case, since neither vitamin shots, nor herbal restorers, had any effect. She remained with Alexandra – and in that state, she was physically present, but far away from both me and real life. Somebody who is that far away from it all, is not hungry and you can watch them lose weight, because they only hunger for the beloved person who has been lost forever.

As a doctor, I was a failure, because my healing techniques had been totally useless and had gone up in smoke. It was a tragedy, because among all the people I knew, I could not help the person closest to me. It was wearing me down. It took away my self-confidence. I had already been down enough after Alexandra's death, but now I was being dragged down even further. For a while, I had given up – myself, my marriage, even my wife Petra.

During the first year following Alexandra's death, our days were dull and unhappy, because we both lived in a dark and unhappy world of our own. Petra did not withdraw as much as I did, but she did not want a lot of publicity while in that state. One time, she watched the ballet Swan Lake. During the scene where the queen bent over her dead son, she had to cry bitterly. At a birthday dinner to which she had been invited, she burst into tears at the thought that Alexandra would never celebrate another birthday.

Alexandra was, and still is, ever present in Petra's mind – and I guess she always will be, together with the grief and pain. But the changes I have seen since the summer of 2003 still give me hope and confirm my statement that NADH is not only a restorer for the brain, but also for the soul and the mind.

This has been proven by the studies mentioned in the medical section later in this book. However, despite of all the studies, the most important thing for a doctor is to be able to experience and witness for himself how a natural remedy can give a person new vitality and joy of life within a few weeks.

I have used the metaphor of the classic change of a weather pattern in the mountains to explain Petra's dark moments with all of their dangers. Since Petra has been taking the nutritive substance NADH every morning, the wind has virtually changed in her (as well as in my) life. The dark clouds have disappeared. Finally, the sky is clear and blue again and our lives are full of sunlight. Petra is doing the same things that she did in the months before, but she is doing them with a lot of delight and pleasure. Things seem to work more easily and smoothly, because she has a positive and life-affirming attitude. Petra looks rejuvenated and radiant.

When I look into my darling Petra's eyes and face today, I can see more and more joy and less and less grief and pain. That is what I am grateful for.

How I discovered NADH for us

You have read how my wife and I were in a deep crisis after Alexandra's death. For about 18 months, I was completely unable to do anything useful. Petra was more active, but in her own way unhappy, in fact, she was absolutely devastated. However, as the disciplined person that I have always admired, she forced herself to return to her desk where, during an actually useless time of our lives, she produced her book "Und eine Nacht vergeht wie ein Jahr" ("And one night passes like a year" – only available in German - translator's note). It is based on Petra's recordings and became a bestseller. As far as I am concerned, I did not produce anything during those months, at least nothing that might have seriously helped to pull us out of that situation.

It was not until February 2003 that I became active. It was rather a coincidence that I received a call from a former colleague. We chatted about how things were going, what we were doing and about all the banalities that are deemed to be part of polite conversation. This colleague still had his own medical practice in Munich. He is about 20 years younger than I am, and very committed to his job. His name does not matter in this context, but what does matter is something that – in between a general running down of current politics and moaning about the weather – he planted into my ear. He said – and that electrified me – "Just imagine, Dr. Müller (a colleague well-known to both of us) fought his depression and his long-lasting fatigue syndrome in no more than 4 weeks with Co-Enzyme 1, i.e. by taking the nutritional substance NADH."

I did not want to sound stupid or otherwise signal to my colleague that, as a pensioner, I was not up-to-date with current medicine. So with some scepticism in my voice, I said: "Oh, really? That is absolutely amazing; we can only congratulate Mueller on this". My answer was just blah blah, simply because I did not have the guts to ask what I was dying to know at that moment. It was the question, what actually is Co-Enzyme 1, or NADH?

No sooner had I put down the receiver, than I rushed over to Petra who was sitting in her study writing down her memoirs. I asked her if she had ever heard about Co-Enzyme 1, or NADH. Petra is an enzyme expert. In order to retain her good figure, she had thoroughly researched the subject of enzymes and had used TRI-S-ZYM diets from the chemist's over many years. On top of that, she had written a book about how to lose weight with enzymes. She knew about Co-Enzyme Q10 that can be of value to the heart. Nevertheless, she knew just as little about Co-Enzyme 1 as I did.

Since I had not only been a doctor, but also an editor in a well-known publishing house for many years, we have a large and comprehensive library in our home. There was not one single encyclopaedia in which I could find the keyword "Co-Enzyme" or even "Co-Enzyme 1". I did find something about enzymes though - which was this:

> *"Enzymes are high-molecular proteins that are produced in living cells of plants or animals and that often have a complicated structure. Enzymes enable or speed up a number of chemical reactions in the body required for the modification and decomposition of working material and nutrients. The enzymes function mainly by temporarily bonding with the participants of this reaction, without being modified themselves during that reaction. If one enzyme is missing, or is blocked, due to abnormal transformation, the normal procedure of the metabolic processes will be disrupted. Various enzymes consist of two components, i.e. the apo-enzyme which facilitates the sensitivity of a substrate and the co-enzyme which is responsible for its effectiveness."*

Even though I am a physician, I could not make any sense of this. Repentant of my ignorance, I called my friend the next day to ask him to explain to me what are Co-Enzyme 1 and NADH and what the patients in his practice had experienced with this substance.

On the next few pages, I am going to describe what he explained to me in a long telephone conversation. It was his subjective, but also very enthusiastic, first-hand report that, several weeks later, made me try out this remedy, which is completely natural and free from side effects, on myself.

Here is my colleague's report.

Experiences of a befriended doctor

NADH is a co-enzyme, which increases the catalysing effect of many different enzymes in our body. Just a few milligrams of NADH in our body can often lead to dramatic improvement of a particular problem. If we strengthen our body with NADH, or Co-Enzyme 1, day after day, many wonderful and healthy things will happen.

<u>NADH lowers the blood pressure.</u> A double blind study performed in the USA revealed that after taking NADH for 11 weeks (one pill of 5 milligrams a day), high blood pressure was lowered by at least 30% and almost automatically levelled off at a normal value.

<u>NADH helps with Parkinson's disease</u>. Many studies have shown that NADH is the ideal supplement for shaking palsy (Parkinson's disease). This is no surprise, since NADH is the preliminary stage of dopamine, i.e. the neuro-transmitter that is lacking in Parkinson's patients.

<u>NADH helps with Alzheimer's disease.</u> Studies made by the George Washington University (USA) have proven that NADH is one of the best remedies to maintain the vitality of the brain. In Alzheimer patients who took three pills of NADH (15 milligrams) per day, the disease was not only stopped, which is what many other medications also do, but NADH did more than that. Brain functions that had been lost came back in many patients.

<u>NADH helps with chronic tiredness</u>. The George Washington University made another study with patients suffering from the so-called Chronic Fatigue Syndrome (chronic tiredness). 80% of all the patients who took three pills of NADH (15 milligrams) per day over a period of six months, recovered. The study was controlled by the US Food and Drug Administration (FDA).

<u>NADH boosts energy levels</u>. Athletes have taken NADH for scientific research. The outcome, in all cases, whether with athletes, footballers, or ice-hockey professionals, was always a rise in energy levels of 50%.

<u>NADH prevents depression</u>. People without energy often get depressed and lethargic. Studies have shown that if a depressive person takes two pills of NADH (10 milligrams) per day, then a significant improvement of their mental condition will show already after 10 to 14 days and that after 4 to 6 weeks, depression and severe mood swings will disappear.

I thanked my colleague for the phone call and while I was hanging up, I knew that I wanted to know a lot more about this miraculous substance. And it had to be real quick. Because from the first moment on, I had a premonition that NADH might help both Petra and me. And that is what happened. However, before I actually took NADH and before I gave it to Petra, I spent many weeks reading and researching the subject to get myself thoroughly informed.

I would like to point out one thing though. My wife Petra and I were both greatly helped by NADH. However, there is no guarantee that NADH will help or be useful in every situation. It is like a lock-and-key principle. If the body lacks NADH and a daily dose will supplement it, miracles can happen. If the body does not lack NADH, it will therefore not react to the substance, which will then be excreted without any danger.

Since there are no reliable techniques to measure the level of NADH, we would recommend to just try it out during a critical phase of life, or a phase of weakness. According to all of the findings available so far, NADH has no side effects. There are also no interactions with other drugs. As a precaution, patients who take a lot of medicine should consult their doctor to determine whether they can take NADH.

The following pages are all about NADH. I am going to give an account of what my research and that of some of my colleagues has revealed about Co-Enzyme 1. I have tried to find simple words, even for complex matters, to make them comprehensible for medical laypeople as well. At the end of the book, you will find a comprehensive bibliography, so that experts can be convinced about the accuracy of my statements and about the importance of NADH for people's well-being.

I am going to start with age – and our wish for a long life in the best possible health. In the process of ageing, NADH plays an essential, if not <u>the</u> most essential role.

Everybody wants to get old – but nobody wants to be old!

Why this contradiction? Because for most of us, getting old means degeneration, and this goes along with losing all the functions that make life worth living. Take, for example, our physical health, strength, vitality, mobility and – a threat to many of us – our thinking abilities, or our frame of mind.

Given the choice, most of us would probably opt for the longest possible life – provided we keep fit and well, with a sound mind, while we enjoy our "golden years".

This raises the question: "Why is this not possible?" – After all, we are living in an era characterized by outstanding progress in the fields of medicine and technology! Scientists are able to send human beings to the moon – and thanks to microsurgery, unborn babies can be operated on successfully inside the womb. So, why is the process of ageing still so painful and why have we not yet found a solution to it?

What is indeed remarkable is that within recent years, science has come to some extraordinary conclusions that might decide whether the ageing process of our bodies is good or bad.

Let us, for example, take a look at our brains. Some experts used to believe that our cognitive (mental) functions already begin to degenerate from the age of thirty and that between our mid-sixties and seventies, the brain clearly shows some neurological damage. The latest findings of recent years have shown, however, that our mental capacity is not necessarily doomed to decline due to ageing. If appropriate measures are taken, there is no plausible reason why any of our mental skills should be impaired.

If this sounds like "science fiction" to you, then let me refer to a recognized scientific formula to calculate the possible age of mammals. According to this formula, the number of years a skeleton takes to be fully-grown should be multiplied by 5. The skeleton of a human (which is scientifically included amongst the mammals) is fully-grown by the age of 25.

Now, if we multiply this figure by 5, this means a lifetime of 125 years! The reason why only a small number of people in industrialized countries live to such an old age can be found in a number of harmful factors that are caused by our modern lifestyle. These factors also have a negative overall effect on our immune system and on the DNA (genetics) of our body cells.

It is obvious that good health and longevity are dependent on a number of factors like lifestyle, exercise and, most importantly, nutrition. Nutrition not only means a balanced diet with a lot of fresh food, fruit and vegetables – even though these products obviously play a vital role in the upkeep of optimum health and vitality. What is crucial, however, is the quality and quantity of those nutritional components without which life could not be sustained. The vitality and functioning of our cells and that of our whole organism are dependent on vitamins, mineral nutrients, enzymes and co-enzymes.

Only when our cells receive all of the required nutrients in the optimum proportions, can these protect our body from infection, deposits and diseases that would otherwise enhance our ageing process.

What exactly is the reason for ageing?

Because research and science have found out more about the functioning of our body at the cellular level, it has been clearly shown that ageing is mainly a result of cellular death and the degeneration of tissue. If we can stop this process – in fact, we finally seem to understand how this can be achieved – then we will eventually be able to improve health as a whole and this will lead to a longer life.

According to recent research findings, approximately 70% of all cancerous diseases, more than 50% of all heart diseases and almost all cases of osteoporosis could be prevented by a change in lifestyle and by an appropriate diet. And this is just the beginning. We only need to think of other diseases that we associate with ageing, e.g. memory loss, Alzheimer's and Parkinson's disease, etc. It seems that even if these diseases have already broken out, the addition of certain key nutritional substances to the diet can contribute a lot to slow down the progression of an illness or to stop it, or – in some cases – the condition can even be improved.

The ageing process begins at the lowest level of our lives, i.e. in our body cells. Consequently, if we want to slow down the ageing process, we have to pay a lot of attention to supplying the cells with suitable nutrients.

One of the most important components in this process is the hardly known co-enzyme called NADH that has a complicated structure (enzymes are macromolecular protein compounds, which speed up biochemical processes, or make them possible in the first place). What this substance is all about, how it was discovered and – most importantly – how it can help fight disease, bad health and premature ageing, will be explained in this book.

If you want to stay young and live longer – without being afflicted by degenerative and painful disease – don't miss out on NADH, which might play an important part in inhibiting the ageing process and protecting you from disease.

NADH – The anti-ageing enzyme

Physicians and biologists would probably find it difficult to define one specific endogenous substance as being the "most important" one. On the other hand, they can hardly dismiss the fact that the co-enzyme NADH comes pretty close to fulfilling that requirement. Then how is it that so little has been heard of that substance, although NADH was identified as an essential substance for the body many years ago? The reason is probably that until some years ago, there was no known method to increase the concentration of NADH in the cells. So why talk about something that cannot be influenced?

Luckily, this changed in the early 90s when Professor Dr. Dr. Georg D. Birkmayer, an Austrian scientist, developed the substance NADH in tablet form. Dr. Birkmayer is a world-famous researcher in the biochemical field who was the first to identify the importance of NADH for the development of cells and the transport of energy to all body functions and organs.

He was the medical director of the Birkmayer Institute for the therapy of Parkinson's disease in Vienna, in which thousands of patients suffering from Parkinson's, Alzheimer's and depression have already been treated. Dr. Birkmayer is the author of more than 150 research papers and more than 100 scientific articles in the area of neuro-chemistry and neuro-pharmacology in connection with

Parkinson's and Alzheimer's disease. He is a professor at Graz University, a visiting professor at Beijing University and General Secretary of the International Academy of Tumour Marker Oncology, New York.

Dr. Birkmayer gave NADH to his patients at the institute in Vienna that he was running. In various different disease patterns like Parkinson's, Alzheimer's and depression, it was demonstrated that a complementary medication of NADH was advantageous. The benefit of this amazing substance with respect to the disorders mentioned, as well as the highly impressive results achieved in the treatment of chronic fatigue disorder, will be discussed later in this book.

I must point out now, however, that not only the people who suffer from one of the illnesses described above will benefit from this "magic bullet" from the world of dietary supplements! NADH can also be used to raise everybody's general energy levels and improve their well-being – irrespective of age and current health conditions! But not only that – more and more experts on old age consider NADH to be an extremely helpful supplement and that means for everyone who is interested in staying young and who wants to feel vital and healthy up to a ripe old age. In a nutshell: NADH is one of the first and most important supplements against premature ageing that will ever be launched on the market!

How to stay younger and have a longer life – thanks to NADH

As with other essential vitamins, minerals and nutrients, our body is not capable of producing NADH by itself. Nevertheless, a sufficient quantity of this vital co-enzyme was available to us already at birth and, in a perfect world, we would all be able to fulfil the current requirement by means of a normal diet. The problem of modern nutrition is, however, that due to a number of conditions that will be discussed later, most of our food has been depleted of nutritional value and therefore does not even come close to supplying the required quantity of NADH.

Fortunately, this requirement can now be satisfied by taking additional NADH. This will raise the total level of energy running through the trillions of cells that form our body and may consequently lead to a longer lifetime. Of course, the natural process of ageing, which is an unalterable fact of life, cannot be avoided. However, the good news is: NADH can prevent all of the symptoms commonly connected with ageing that are simply accepted and more or less expected to be part of the ageing process.

NADH is responsible for many vital processes in the brain and in the body, including maintenance of memory, mental alertness and the ability to make decisions. Moreover, it can enhance sexual activity, brighten up one's mood, increase physical strength and much more. Therefore, NADH not only extends your life – it also helps you to have more pleasure in life! It has also been observed that NADH has an appetite suppressant effect, i.e. it helps to avoid excessive eating. Therefore, it is most helpful for those who have problems keeping their weight.

To understand more about the pivotal effect of NADH in fighting disease and slowing down the ageing process – and why taking additional NADH could be a special benefit for you – let us take a look at the important metabolic qualities that this co-enzyme has on our bodies:

On top of the list is the primary role of NADH to produce energy in every living cell. Therefore, supplementing your nutrition with NADH provides a greatly enhanced source of additional cellular - and therefore basic – energy.

For an ongoing production of healthy and efficient cells, the human body needs to have a faultless and healthy DNA (the genetic plan contained in the cell nucleus). Unfortunately, the DNA can and often will be attacked from the outside. NADH plays a fundamental role in repairing the DNA.

For a number of reasons – most of all through chemotherapy – cells may be damaged; in those cases, NADH is essential for the repair and replacement of cells.

We all need NADH in order to defend ourselves successfully against disease. It has been shown that taking a supplement of NADH in addition to a normal diet will strengthen the immune system.

Every living organism needs anti-oxidants in order to fight against the threat of potentially harmful free radicals. The damage caused by so-called "villains" is thought to trigger approximately 80 different diseases. Among all known anti-oxidants, NADH is deemed to be the most potent anti-oxidant.

Our brains produce chemical substances that are required for our memory, thinking, the judgment of general well-being and many others. Research has shown that thanks to NADH, it is possible for us to produce these so-called neurotransmitters, which are sometimes insufficient in our bodies. This can be especially important for people suffering from depression.

Who needs NADH?

The main subject of this book is a dietary supplement that is based on an enzyme with stunning anti-oxidative qualities which releases energy. It may therefore be useful to explain briefly, in which cases we should actually take dietary supplements.

We are all different. Some people have special dietary needs that can be covered by special additives; for others, a precautionary intake may be beneficial. Many experts in the public health sector agree today that a large number of health problems are caused by an unbalanced intake of nutrients.

It is certainly not a new idea that a balanced nutrition is important for a healthy body. However, it is becoming more and more obvious today that some so-called healthy diets by no means come up to our basic dietary needs. For many years, we have been encouraged to eat healthy, natural, well-balanced and fresh food – and by and large, this is what we did!

Over the years, we, as the consumers, have put a lot of pressure on the market and thereby forced the retailers to make the so-called "organic products" more and more available, and producers and suppliers have fulfilled that demand. However, the result was not what we had actually expected, because some of the food we buy only seems to be balanced. As a matter of fact, the food was not only grown in low-nutrient soil, but – due to the industrial-scale processing and manufacturing methods - it has also lost a lot of valuable nutrients which we had hoped to find in it.

Intensive agriculture, food technology, artificial fertilizers, pesticides and the cost pressure that farmers are facing, has led to the fact that what ends up on our plates is the result of economic, rather than health- and environment-focussed decisions. It is sad enough to realize that many food producers are more anxious to fill their pockets with good money, rather than to fill our stomachs with good products. A drastic depletion of natural vitamins and minerals in our food means that, unless we take nutrient supplements, we will suffer a significant lack of vital nutrients.

The de-mineralization of our soils (due to environmental pollution and intensive agriculture) has obviously led to a de-mineralization of our food and, subsequently, to a lack of minerals in our body tissue. Various parties have claimed that this may well be the reason for a large number of modern-day diseases and ailments.

Agricultural products are depleted in nutrients already before they reach the storehouses of large producers and are depleted even more by further processing. This leads to completely low-nutrient and virtually de-natured finished products. Although these "unnatural" products may well fill our stomachs and satisfy our hunger, our organisms will feel deceived by the large number of "empty" calories that contain no essential nutrients.

NADH is contained in every cell of living organisms, including plants and animals. Therefore, NADH should be part of our daily food. Although people who eat meat could be better off than vegetarians, since meat contains more NADH than vegetables and other vegetarian food, it is widely accepted that both vegetarians and meat eaters gradually come to suffer from a lack of NADH.

Why is that so? It is because the NADH that is ingested with the food was either lost through cooking the meal, or else it will be prematurely degraded by the gastric acid while still in the digestive tract.

Compared to your car, this lack of essential nutrients would have the following impact: With diluted petrol, your car would not even start, and even if it did, it would not run properly and suffer damage. Now, if you were to find out what kind of petrol you had been sold – would it not matter to you, or would you go back to the filling station and complain? In the same way as you want to fill your car with only high-quality petrol, your body also deserves only the best of food, unless you agree to live in an ailing, weary system that threatens to break down some day.

Even if you are in perfect health, selectively enriching your nutrition provides a relatively cheap and reliable health insurance. It is a fact that every "body" deserves to receive dietary supplements of only the highest quality. Supplements can generally improve fitness and well-being, protect people against premature ageing and support the immune system. Many people feel more vital, more healthy and stronger when taking supplements. In conclusion, it can be claimed that it always makes sense to take high-quality supplements.

What is an anti-oxidant?

As has already been mentioned, NADH is the most effective biological anti-oxidant. Therefore, let us take a closer look at what an anti-oxidant actually is and what it does.

It is widely accepted that anti-oxidants are beneficial for the maintenance of a healthy immune system, as well as for the long-term integrity of body cells and tissues. Anti-oxidants attack the potentially dangerous substances called "free radicals" and render them harmless. These are formed in the body during common metabolic processes and when fighting disease. Free radicals contain unpaired electrons, which, once they have been released, will search for other molecules with which to react. This reaction is called oxidation (oxidation means chemical decomposition, e.g. the rusting of iron), and it can damage the DNA and the cell walls. This may have negative effects and trigger the outbreak of disease.

To understand how anti-oxidants work, we first have to take a look at the oxidizing agent which is oxygen. As we all know, there is no way that we can live without oxygen. Without breathing, nothing works. When we breathe, oxygen passes into our blood and will then transported to our cells.

When it is absorbed in the cells, oxygen is essential for a number of important processes that happen in our cells. On the other hand, the same oxygen in the form of free oxygen radicals can oxidize our tissue. In other words, it can cause our tissue to "rust". Oxygen waste products, called lipofuscin, may accumulate in the organs, such as the heart and the brain, leading to a brown discoloration of the tissue. These spots are a sign of ageing, and they will become more and more noticeable as we get older.

To understand this process, let us imagine an apple. If you cut it up into slices and expose the slices to the air, they will go brown. Due to the oxygen contained in the air, the surface of the apple slices will oxidize. This process is similar to what happens when free oxygen radicals are formed in our bodies. In contrast, if we sprinkle lemon juice, which is rich in vitamin C and has the effect of an anti-oxidant, onto the apple slices, they will not change colour. Lemon juice will stop the oxidation process and prevent the apple from "rusting". Anti-oxidants do exactly the same thing in our bodies.

Oxidation causes our arteries to age, and this can make them fragile. Each one of our body cells contains DNA (deoxyribonucleic acid) which tells the cell what to do and what not to do. With every cell division, the DNA is copied into the newly formed cell. Oxidation disturbs this process and leads to damage in the DNA. This can cause cancerous disease and premature ageing of tissue structures.

In the same way, the immune system can be damaged, and the eyes may age because of a damage to the lenses (cataract) and the retina.

Anti-oxidants not only protect us – they also help our immune system to fight against disease that already exists. Our immune system is a highly effective defence mechanism, unless it has been weakened by environmental influences. Anti-oxidants support common immunological processes and help to revive them after a recent illness.

Stimulation of the immune system by the addition of anti-oxidants to food is of increasing interest for the prevention and perhaps even the cure of cancer. Experimental studies have shown, that healthy people who developed cancer later on, had a lower level of anti-oxidative substances in their organisms compared to those who remained in good health.

You may have heard of other well-known anti-oxidants like the vitamins A, C and E and the micro-nutrient selenium.

Something you are probably not aware of is the fact that NADH not only shows a much greater anti-oxidative potential than these, it reputedly works as a "super substance" among natural anti-oxidants. Apparently, the other anti-oxidants are also regenerated by NADH, so that they can fight against pathogenic free radicals. Only a few molecules of this super-substance are necessary to initiate a chain reaction, so that used vitamin C can be transformed into active vitamin C. What is even more remarkable is that NADH can achieve the same results with vitamin E.

Of course, free radicals not only have disadvantages. As always, it is only a question of balance! As has been stated earlier, in the course of the natural process of oxidation metabolism in the body, a small number of free radicals will be formed in the body as unavoidable by-products. However, problems will arise when there is an unbalanced quantity of anti-oxidants and free radicals in the body. This can be compared to a football match in which one team has more players than the other. The smaller team will probably become tired much sooner, because the players have to do more running in order to keep their adversaries under control, while the larger team will get more scoring chances. Hence, the smaller team uses up more energy and has to make up for it through an additional supply of energy. The situation is similar when an additional supply of anti-oxidants is needed.

Many other external factors increase our exposure to free oxygen radicals. These include: alcohol, cigarette smoke, traces of pollutants and heavy metals – as found in food and water – UV radiation and other types of high-energy radiation, stress and drugs, e.g. antibiotics. As hard as we may try to avoid burdening our lives with pollutants, it is hardly possible for us to escape these sources of disturbance.

When our bodies are attacked by these external factors, it may over-react and thus raise the production of free radicals to a dangerous level. The problems start when we are not any more capable of producing enough anti-oxidants to balance out the surplus of free radicals. If these free radicals are left to reproduce freely, this can make way for the development of heart disease, cancer, Parkinson's and Alzheimer's, allergies, arthritis and many other known diseases of civilization. In other words, we can be attacked by our own metabolism!

As already mentioned, oxidation can damage the DNA and the cell walls and thereby open the door to illness and disease. The damage caused can take different forms: fat oxidation (going rancid); reactive melting of molecules; making it impossible for the cells to take up nutrients and to dispose of waste materials; tearing apart cell membranes causing a leakage of essential cell components – which mostly leads to the death of cells or tissue. Thanks to their chemical properties, anti-oxidants can prevent this by immediately reacting with oxygen. This enables them to inhibit the detrimental oxidation process from the start. Fortunately, it is possible to protect your own body by supplying it with high-quality anti-oxidants like NADH.

Anti-oxidants like NADH are truly our best friends, since they also stimulate our immune system.

As long as they are not busy catching free radicals on the biological "battlefield", anti-oxidants will work at home where they help to strengthen our natural defence system, when it is necessary to ward off existing, or oncoming, illness.

There is another theory according to which anti-oxidants – and NADH in particular – could be extremely effective in the fight against premature ageing. It is said that cells start ageing when the DNA repair mechanism does not work efficiently any more. To repair the DNA, however, NADH is necessary, but its availability diminishes with age. Furthermore, many of the continuous attacks to the cellular DNA are caused by free radicals. NADH also provides an anti-oxidative effect here by targeting these dangerous invaders.

What is NADH?

Every living cell, whether from the realm of animals, or plants, whether it is a single bacteriua, or a cell in our bodies, contains nicotinamide adenine dinucleotide hydride (NADH), a co-enzyme that is indispensable for the production of cellular energy. Animal cells produce and contain more NADH, because animals need more energy to move, while plants hardly move at all and therefore contain much less NADH (This is also the reason why vegetarians often suffer from a lack of NADH – and can benefit considerably from a daily intake from a supplementary diet!) The highest concentration of NADH can be found in body organs that are very active, or use up a lot of energy, like the brain, or muscular cells. Cells in the human heart muscle contain a remarkable 90 micrograms of NADH per kg of tissue. This ultimately enables the cells to contract every second, in fact for a whole lifetime – 3600 times every hour! In comparison, a potato cell is not as diligent. It only contains 0.2 micrograms per kg.

We are all born with a sufficient quantity of NADH and are then forced to satisfy our needs through the food we eat, because NADH – like several other vital substances – cannot be produced by the body itself. A lack of nutrients in our food, or an insufficient absorption of nutrients, however, can lead to a lack of NADH and – because the production of energy will then decrease steadily from one cell to another – this may lead to a state of general weakness, or even illness.

Enzymes act as catalysts in biological processes, in order to produce substances (molecules) that the body needs for its survival. One could compare this with a machine used in a production process that transforms one material into another by applying a particular procedure. Or alternatively, with petrol that is filled into the tank of a car. This will be transformed into energy and thus make the vehicle move. Inside of the body, enzymes act as catalysts to the process of breaking up food into small, useful particles of water and energy, in order to "run" the body. However, an enzyme is only as good as the co-enzyme with which it collaborates! It is only with the help of co-enzymes that enzymes can do their jobs. In the same way as a car needs petrol.

Once the food has been digested, the individual components will be transported into the cells with the help of another enzyme, to a place where the co-enzyme NADH is active and where it transforms the components into a form of energy called ATP (adenosine triphosphate) – (for more details see a later section). NADH ignites the spark that the engine needs to start. A lack of NADH, on the other hand, leads to a lack of energy on a cellular level, causing the symptom of tiredness. The body then feels like a car that has run out of petrol – and who has not experienced that at some point in their lives? The more NADH the cells of our body have available, the more energetic we will feel. Unfortunately, as we have already mentioned, the quantity of NADH decreases with age and the same applies to the enzymes that depend on NADH – especially those that are responsible for the supply of energy.

In other words, an enzyme that is produced by the body itself will only be able to actually do its work if it has a sufficient quantity of co-enzyme available which, however, the body is not able to produce on its own. Because these are not found in our food in a quantity that we would like to have and in connection with the fact that there is no life without ageing, we must conclude that it is becoming increasingly difficult for us to satisfy our need for NADH. That is the reason why we can all benefit from dietary products that "energize" us.

What is the actual effect of NADH?

Scientists first discovered NADH in yeast 90 years ago, and a lot has been written about it in biochemical teaching books ever since. It was not until recently though that it was produced in a form that could be used as a dietary supplement. We now expect to hear a lot more about it in the near future.

Due to the increased energy output of each individual body cell, one can benefit from more energy being available. This can lead to improvements in the following areas:

- Stamina and endurance – both physically and mentally!
- Regulation of the cholesterol level in the blood, blood pressure and the reproduction of cells.
- Immune system
- The ability to repair damaged DNA, which might otherwise lead to degenerative diseases.
- Quick and effective ability of the body to repair damaged or "worn-out" cells.
- Memory and psychological well-being – especially depression, since NADH stimulates the production of brain substances (neuro-transmitters).
- Many conditions, both psychological and physical, commonly regarded as symptoms of old age.

NADH provides the cells with the energy that they need in order to stay alive – in the end it keeps us alive. Without energy, every cell will die and a large heap of cells would be the only thing that is left of us! A supplementary intake of NADH is, therefore, a simple method to supply the cells with the energy that they need in order to improve our mental and physical energy. So who could not live with that?

To get a better picture of the actual effects of NADH, we need to have a basic understanding of how our body produces energy. In simple terms, our body needs two things to stay alive and these are food (glucose) and air (oxygen). We then use a process called cellular breathing, in order to transform these two vital substances into an energy carrier called ATP (adenosine triphosphate, which is the primary intra-cellular source of energy). Each cell needs this energy in the form of ATP – it makes the heart cells beat, the lung cells breathe, the brain cells think and it keeps us generally alive!

We must now get a little more technical and take a closer look at how this process actually works. After a meal, the body stores the digested food as glycogen, which will then be transformed into glucose molecules to satisfy our immediate need for energy. This glucose becomes a sort of fuel that is required to release energy into the body so that our cells can do the job that they were destined to do from birth. N a similar way, when a car is filled with petrol, the engine will not function as long as the spark plugs do not ignite the fuel and finally get the engine going

– this is exactly what NADH does: It ignites the fuel-air mixture which produces the pressure that is needed to finally make the wheels turn.

The human body is a type of "combustion engine". It needs energy to be able to function. It needs to breathe, eat and sleep. Our body is an unbelievably complicated system built of about 70 trillion cells – a number that most of us will find hard to imagine! In order to keep alive, each one of these cells must produce energy – that is why we have to eat and breathe. Each of these cells contains mitochondria in which this energy is produced. Mitochondria are the power plants of the cells. Cells work together in groups, which form the various parts of the body, each with a specific function. Each individual cell gets instructions about the role it has to play within the whole system, which are archived in the DNA (deoxyribonucleic acid).

Each power station within the individual cell produces the same form of energy – the ATP molecule. It is this process that is responsible for enabling our body to make use of the air that we breathe. Oxygen is required for nothing else other than the production of ATP. Each mitochondrion contains many engines that take in air, burn it and release it in the form of carbon dioxide and water. Once ignited by NADH, the fuel will burn and produce heat in the body. The extent to which, or the speed at which, these engines work defines what we understand to be metabolism (the influence on metabolism). Rapid engines are available for fast metabolic reactions and slow engines for unhurried ones. Similar to the supply of oxygen and glucose, NADH is carried into the cell from outside through food that is delivered from the outside world. You will now begin to recognize why a sufficient supply of NADH is of vital importance and why we cannot ignore the fact that it is not simply available on the supermarket shelves, even though this would be more convenient.

NADH repairs damaged DNA

DNA (deoxyribonucleic acid) is a term that most of us have already heard about. But do we really know what it is? Let us just take a closer look at it.

DNA is the cell's archive. It is in charge of the contents and the safe storage of genetic information within the cell. This is the information that exactly defines to what type of cell it applies and what its function is. It is DNA that exactly determines our identity and the qualities that make us unique. We can say that it is responsible for who we are, as it carries our building plan.

DNA is so fundamental that this genetic material absolutely must remain unchanged. Only in this way, can it be guaranteed that after our cells divide the next generation of cells will be created in exactly the same form as those from which they stem. If the DNA is altered, due to some external chemical, or physical, influence, the newly formed "baby cells" can be different from the parent cells – and will therefore no longer function in the same way.

Unfortunately, we are frequently exposed to chemicals in our homes, at our workplaces, or in our free time, without being aware of how dangerous these substances could be. Perhaps one would prefer not to know it, but the chemical industry produces about 20,000 new compounds per year! Some of them are put into use without an exact knowledge about their toxic effects on certain organisms. We should also not forget that most of these substances are used in laboratories, or similar places, far away from the public! It has been acknowledged that by far the largest number of toxins that harm the environment are chemical substances used in the household, or at work! Harmful toxins may react with our DNA and, once that has been damaged, our genetic material may be changed. This could be the basis for the development of Parkinson's, Alzheimer's, cancer, loss of memory, rheumatoid arthritis and chronic fatigue, to name but a few of the degenerative conditions that we are afraid to face in old age. Furthermore, some of these diseases may manifest themselves years after the actual contact with the toxin took place.

Luckily, the human body possesses a system of its own that can repair the DNA. It has been recognized that NADH plays a key role in this process. Studies have shown that the DNA repair system improves with the NADH level in the body. In other words, NADH is an extremely important "instrument" in our biological toolbox.

NADH helps patients with chronic fatigue syndrome

The chronic fatigue syndrome (CFS) is an extremely impeding dysfunction of unknown cause for which there is no known cure. Therefore, it is a highly welcome discovery that NADH can improve the situation of hundreds of thousands of affected people worldwide. The possibility that CFS could be caused by a shortfall of energy from ATP is currently being examined at various health centres and, so far, there have been positive signs. As explained in the chapter "What is the actual effect of NADH?", ATP is the energy source that is produced in every cell by cellular breathing, a process that can only be initiated by NADH. A lack of ATP expresses itself as excessive fatigue, feebleness and muscular pain. What is more, taking a break does not lead to improvement, or regeneration, whereas every minor effort brings about even greater exhaustion. The CFS patient is all too familiar with these symptoms.

Clinical investigations have shown that CFS patients taking NADH supplements reported that they felt less tired and, at the same time, had more strength and stamina, as well as experiencing a boost in their mental energy. Another piece of good news is that NADH is non-toxic and can be taken along with medicines without any unwanted side effects.

CFS is characterized by a combination of various symptoms and cannot be described very precisely, whereas other diseases may be determined with 100% certainty. There is no standardized examination that clearly defines whether or not the patient suffers from CFS. It is therefore difficult to diagnose and makes the ailment one of the most often falsely diagnosed illnesses. In recent years, doctors at the American Centre for Disease Control have used trial methods to establish a list of criteria that will ensure a safer diagnosis of CFS.

Criteria of CFS:

- Fatigue continuing for more than 6 months
- Dry throat
- Hardened lymph nodes
- Inexplicable muscle and joint pains
- Fatigue continuing more than 24 hours after exertion
- Headache
- Disturbances of the short-term memory, forgetfulness and lack of concentration
- Sleep disorders

CFS is certainly not a new disease. First cases were reported more than 100 years ago. Over time, CFS has been given various names, such as "yuppie flu", "Epstein-Barr syndrome", or "chronic fatigue", as well as CFIDS ("chronic fatigue immune dysfunction syndrome").

In certain medical circles, it is even believed that CFS might reach epidemic proportions within the next century. Studies have shown that many patients developed CMS symptoms after a viral infection, or after going through a particularly stressful experience. Alarmingly, an increasing number of cases in children and adolescents have been reported. Most of these cases concern people with previous allergies, or other diseases that made it necessary to take strong antibiotics. Please refer once again to the chapter "What is an anti-oxidant?", in which it is explained how some types of antibiotics may increase the number of free radicals in the body – and how NADH can work efficiently as an anti-oxidant to eliminate these potentially harmful chemicals and thereby prevent the risk of harm. This is another good reason why we should supplement our food and that of our children with NADH!

NADH and Parkinson's disease

Now let us take a look at Parkinson's and find out what kind of disease it actually is. For many years, Parkinson's was considered to be a disease which is typical of old age. This opinion had to be revised, however, when it became publicly known that the young actor Michael J. Fox had been diagnosed with Parkinson's. Parkinson's is a degenerative disorder of the brain that expresses itself by trembling lips and hands and by cramped muscles. At an advanced stage, the whole body is trembling, the gait is sluggish, or at worst, moving forward is completely impossible.

Parkinson's breaks out when brain cells that are meant to produce dopamine (Dopamine is a neurotransmitter without which the central nervous system cannot function) die. Fortunately, research has shown that NADH enhances the production of dopamine and stimulates the tyrosinhydroxylase (TH) enzyme, which plays a key role in the production of dopamine. A leading study covering a large number of Parkinson's patients who were given NADH was carried out at a German university hospital and it showed that the patients had a higher level of dopamine in the blood. This could well be a substantial argument for treating this disease with NADH.

A classical medicine for the treatment of Parkinson's is Sinemet™, a combination product that contains L-dopa and decarboxylase. This treatment was originally introduced in 1961 by Dr. Georg Birkmayer's father, Walter Birkmayer. As mentioned in the introduction, the physician and scientist Georg D. Birkmayer was the first to discover the importance of NADH and to make it available as a dietary supplement.

Therapy with Sinemet™ is based on substitution. In other words, it makes dopamine available from the outside as a substitute for when the brain does not produce a sufficient quantity. By taking L-dopa, many patients are freed from their symptoms; they become less stiff and more mobile. But L-dopa also has some disadvantages. In particular, it reduces the activity of the natural enzyme inherent in the body, which normally produces dopamine. Thus, while it artificially fills the gap, it prevents our own body from balancing out the deficiency by itself. Another disadvantage of a treatment with L-dopa is the way in which it is absorbed by the body. This means that the whole body and the brain need to be flooded with a very large quantity of L-dopa and dopamine – and this procedure causes the production of a huge quantity of free radicals which could then be even more harmful to the areas of the brain that are already degenerated.

Because of the disadvantages of a conventional treatment as mentioned above, NADH has received more attention, since it stimulates the human body to produce L-dopa by itself in a natural way and thereby makes it unnecessary to fill up this deficiency with drugs. Various investigations have shown the efficiency of NADH in improving mobility – sometimes after only two weeks with a daily intake of 5 mg.

In the meantime, NADH has been given to thousands of patients suffering from Parkinson's disease, with an overwhelming majority experiencing considerable improvement. This occurred particularly after an oral intake rather than after injection, which was used in a few cases. The pronounced anti-oxidative effect of NADH is also important when using it as a remedy for the prevention of this threatening disease, since a surplus of free radicals could be a reason for the development of this and other neurodegenerative disorders! To sum up:

A supplementary intake of NADH, which is the strongest natural anti-oxidant, can play an important role in preventing this or some other debility.

NADH and Alzheimer's disease

Alzheimer's disease is a menacing disease that afflicts many families and can sometimes almost destroy them. It is a neuro-degenerative illness of the brain cells and it afflicts millions of elderly people over the age of 65 worldwide. Its cause is largely unknown and there is no cure. The symptoms include a gradual loss of memory, disorientation, a decreasing capacity for judgment, personality change and a loss of communication skills. Someone who is affected by this horrible disease can change so radically that it may become hard for friends to recognize him/her at all! Since NADH has shown many remarkable capabilities, because it is atoxic and safe to take together with other medicines, it is certainly a blessing for anyone who is affected by this brain disease, or who is just afraid of getting it, to have it in their medicine chest. NADH has already been proven to give new energy to exhausted brain cells and it can help to enhance the fresh supply of chemical neuro-transmitters in the brain. As a highly effective anti-oxidant, it is also known to combat neuro-degenerative illnesses and to fulfil an important task in repairing cells and the DNA, as well as to strengthen the immune system. All of these are benefits that make NADH recommendable also as a remedy to support the fight against Alzheimer's disease.

A scientific study of Alzheimer's patients with a loss of memory, which involved a supplementary intake of NADH, showed measurable improvements. As a result, another study has been launched at the Department of Neurology at the Medical Centre of Georgetown University, USA. The director of studies, Dr. Cohan, stated the following: "NADH is a naturally occurring and well-tolerated compound which has shown promising results in preliminary experiments with Alzheimer's patients. For the time being, there is no treatment or therapy for patients of Alzheimer's approved by the American Food and Drug Administration (FDA), therefore the study mentioned could be a first step towards recognizing that this co-enzyme is possibly of value for Alzheimer's patients."

NADH against depression

It looks as though NADH is nature's primeval anti-depressant. Studies made of patients suffering from depressive symptoms have shown that all of them benefitted from a supplementary intake of NADH! In many cases, depression may be caused by an imbalance in the equilibrium of chemical neuro-transmitters in the brain. Studies have shown that NADH enhances the production of many different neuro-transmitters, such as dopamine, noradrenaline and serotonin. All of these are known to play a role in the outbreak of depressive symptoms.

Dopamine in particular has a positive influence on a number of brain functions, including those that are responsible for the ability to concentrate. It has a positive influence on driving force, libido, the willingness to make decisions and mood. It also helps to control appetite (suppression of ravenousness) and improves sleep. Another piece of good news is that NADH does not show any unwanted interdependencies with other drugs that were prescribed for regular use against depression. It can therefore be taken with maximum security.

Depression is a debilitating disorder that influences both the mental and physical activities, emotions, mood and has a negative influence on general behaviour. Quite often, it completely changes the normal active life of a person.

There are many different symptoms like:
- Joylessness
- Indifference
- Deteriorated concentration
- Insomnia
- Change in appetite
- Compulsive brooding
- General pessimism
- Feeling of guilt and anxiety
- Loss of libido
- Thoughts of suicide

In an experimental study in which NADH was used to treat patients suffering from various depressive symptoms, as many as 93% experienced an improvement.

In the meantime, there is now a large number of patients worldwide who have been taking NADH daily for several years. In addition, many doctors claim that NADH is the most effective anti-depressant substance with which they have ever worked. A further advantage is that to date not one single patient who has taken this supplementary substance has complained about any side effects.

NADH and performance

Scientists recently started to examine the possible use of NADH in connection with athletic performance. Bearing in mind all of the functions of the body that can be supported by NADH, at least theoretically, it seems possible that athletic performance can be improved as well.

NADH is of crucial importance for the energy production in every single one of the trillions of body cells, and a lack of it will inevitably result in some kind of energy deficit. If things do not work perfectly, or near enough at an optimum capacity in just one part of the body, then, just like with an engine, there will be an impact on the rest of the system. This means that there will ultimately be a considerably affect on the overall performance. Because most of the food that we eat is poor in nutrients, most people's "engine" will not run on all cylinders without an appropriate dietary supplement.

A number of competitive cyclists and long distance runners were closely monitored while they were taking NADH to complement their diets. The researchers assessed their reaction times, physical performance and the quality of performance. For comparison purposes, the athletes performed the same tests before and after taking the dietary supplement. The whole series of test was performed after having given them 5 mg of NADH before breakfast for four weeks. During this test phase, the athletes maintained their usual training intensity and frequency and other lifestyle factors, like sleep duration, solid and liquid nutrition, workload, etc.

Four weeks later, most of the athletes showed an improvement in their reaction times, their physical performance, as well as an increase in their maximum intake of oxygen. Some of the improvements might have been due to the fact that the test persons had a lack of NADH before the monitoring started, or because the supplementary intake of NADH stimulated the production of dopamine in the brain – which raised their level of activity and alertness. In any case, the results are self-evident: performance could be improved! It is very likely that an increase in the production of ATP, due to the intake of NADH, eventually resulted in these stunningly enhanced levels of performance.

Another fascinating test was conducted with a top European football team. All footballers were asked to take some additional NADH per day for one month. Blood samples were taken from each player before and after this period, which clearly showed an increase of 30 to 100% in the level of L-dopa after they had taken NADH. As mentioned earlier, L-dopa is transformed in the brain into dopamine, a neuro-transmitter responsible for muscular strength, reaction and instinctive movements, as well as for the emotional and sexual drive. Most of the players also showed an increase in noradrenalin, which improves the level of activity, concentration and the ability to cope with stress. Of course, not only the blood test results spoke for themselves, but the players also reported that they felt better and were much more attentive.

Even if you are not a top athlete, NADH can give you more energy, power, vitality and mental energy. Furthermore, taking a high dose of NADH is neither toxic, nor does it have any undesirable side effects.

Further investigations and clinical tests are under way, so that we can learn more about the full potential of NADH and its influence on the performance of athletes and we will certainly hear more about it in the future! But don't wait for it! Take your supplementary NADH now – and go and get your running shoes!

NADH and the memory

The brain is the command centre of the body. Without our being aware of it, the brain works day and night controlling and co-ordinating all of our body functions. It comprises a huge number of 100 billion neurons, with each one of them being able to contact up to 10,000 other neurons. This makes it possible to build up a complex circuit, which has access to more than 86 billion individual pieces of information per day. Our brains therefore beat the intelligence of any type of computer!

The human brain is designed in such a way that it can absorb information from inside and outside of the body, process and store it - a process that already starts before birth. Without our brains, we would have no past and no future, but only an eternal present – as experienced by people with a pathological memory loss (amnesia). Scientists have been doing research on the brain for many years, probably more profoundly than on any other organ; nevertheless, there is some confusion about how our brains actually work. In some cases, however, experts agree that one of the main preconditions of memory is recognition (the process of receiving signals from the environment through our five senses) and that external stimulation may trigger a reaction in the cells of the central nervous system.

Neuro-transmitters, especially adrenalin, noradrenalin and dopamine, play an important part in all of these processes. If it were possible to increase the production of these substances, then our ability for recognition would be increased accordingly. The enzyme that limits the quantity of dopamine is also capable of storing information. Consequently, a larger quantity of this enzyme should also increase memory performance. Studies have shown that NADH can stimulate the production of this enzyme, as well as that of dopamine. Hence, it should also be able to improve the memory.

As already mentioned in the chapter about NADH and Parkinson's disease, it is considered proven that NADH can raise the dopamine level in the brain. Research has been able to demonstrate that in up to 80% of all patients taking NADH as a dietary supplement, a positive clinical effect on their cognitive performance was observed.

NADH against ageing and disease

We all believe that ageing is unavoidable, since it is a certainty of life. But have you ever thought about what happens biologically when we get older? Ageing is a highly complicated biological process that involves a general decline in the performance of our organs. What we should primarily pay attention to, however, is that ageing involves a gradual reduction of our energy balance. The more we advance in age, the lower our NADH level will get and, along with that, the quantity of energy produced and released in our cells will decrease.

Whenever the energy level in cells drops below a certain threshold value, these cells will die off and the tissue will degenerate. As mentioned earlier in this book, NADH is of major importance in the energy production of all living cells. The more NADH our cells have available, the more energy they can produce, which makes it possible for them and for us as an entity, to stay alive. If there is a sufficient quantity of NADH, the body's own DNA repair system will work at an optimum efficiency, which is an immense help in protecting the body from quite a number of degenerative illnesses, many of which are associated with old age.

Another weapon in the arsenal against ageing is the outstanding capability of NADH as an anti-oxidant. This enables the body to fend off attackers, which occur in the form of free radicals. These attackers can ruin the system, damage cells and open the door to disease.

NADH cannot stop the ageing process completely, but as you get older, you should try to keep the NADH level at that of earlier years. If we all did that, it is quite probable that we would all feel much younger and be active for much longer. What is even more important, we would actively participate in avoiding many illnesses generally associated with old age.

Out of all the achievements that medical research has brought about within recent years, we should consider that the findings concerning the importance of NADH are probably among the most important discoveries. Thanks to this simple dietary supplement, we now have, for the first time, a real opportunity to protect our bodies from ageing and our lives from disease.

Summary

NADH is no longer just a new, hardly studied dietary supplement that is only talked about in scientific circles. In the meantime, it is available to everyone who wants to increase his or her physical or mental energy. A lot has been said in this book about the amazing therapeutic advantages of this vital co-enzyme for patients suffering from chronic, or debilitating diseases like Parkinson's, Alzheimer's, CFS and depression. Nevertheless, it can be beneficial for everyone's body, yours included!

Healthcare is becoming more and more important for all of us, as we recognize more and more our sensitivity towards nutrient deficiency and environmental toxins. Spending money on health insurance is one thing that helps us to get medical treatment in case of an illness. To invest money in NADH, however, is a insurance for our well-being, which might prevent us from needing serious medical treatment in the first place!

As we have said in an earlier chapter, we were all born with a sufficient quantity of NADH. Without any doubt, it was Mother Nature's intention to include all the necessary quantities of NADH in the food that we eat during our lifetimes. Sadly, humanity has contributed a lot towards sabotaging this original plan of Mother Nature. On the other hand, it is slowly occurring to us that a lot of food quite often looks as though it were good for us, but, in fact, it is quite harmful. If we want to keep our physical and mental strength until an advanced old age and the end of our lives, it plainly makes sense to supplement our diet with something that the 60 trillion cells in our body will appreciate – something like NADH.

Sources / Bibliography

Coon MJ. «Oxygen activation in the metabolism of lipids, drugs and carcinogens.» Nutr. Rev. 1978; 36:319-328.

Halliwell B Gutteridge JMC «Oxygen toxicity, oxygen radicals, transition metals and disease.» Biochem. J. 1984; 219:1-14.

Cranton EM and Frankleton JP. «Free radical pathology in ageassociated diseases: Treatment with EDTA chelation, nutrition and anti-oxidants.» J. Hol Med. 1984; 6: 6-36.

Halliwell B Gutteridge JMC. «Role of free radicals catalytic metal ions in human disease: An overview» Methods Enzymol. 1990; 186: 1-85.

Tapel AL. «Lipid peroxidation damage to cell components.» Fed. Proc. 1973; 32: 1870-1874.

Gutteridge JMC, Halliwell B. Antioxidna in Nutrition, Health and Disease. Oxford: Oxford University Press, 1994.

Lehninger, AL. Vitamins and Co-Enzymes, Biochemistry, 2nd Ed.: 337-42: The John Hopkins University School of Medicine, New York: Worth Publishers Inc., 1975.

Alberts B, Bray D, Lewis J, Rff H, Roberts K, Watson JD. «Energy Conversion: Mitochondria and Chloroplasts.» Molekular Biology of the Cell , 3rd Edition: Garland Publishing Inc. 1994; 653-720.

Alberts B, Bray D, Lewis J, Rff H, Roberts K, Watson JD. «Energy Conversion: Mitochondria and Chloroplasts.» Molecular Biology of the Cell , 3rd Edition: Garland Publishing Inc. 1994; 653-720

Devlin, T.M. Biochemistry With Clinical Correlations, 3rd Ed.: 559-63. Hahnemann University School of Medicine, New York: Wiley Liss, 1992.

Fukuda K, Strauss SE, Hickie I et al. «The chronic fatigue syndrome: a comprehensive approach to its definition and study.» Internal Medicine 1994: 212:953-959.

Vrecko K, Birkmayer JGD, Krainz J. «Stimulation of dopamine biosynthesis in culture P12 pheochromocytoma cells by the Co-Enzyme nicotinamide adenide dinucleotide (NADH).» J.Neural. Transm. 1993; 5: 147-156.

Kuhn W Th, Winkel R, Danielczik S, Gerstner A, Hacker R, Mattern C, Przuntek H. «Parenteral application of NADH in Parkinson´s disease: clinical improvement partially due to stimulation of endogenous levodopa biosynthesis». J. Neural. Transm. 1996; 103:1187-1193.

Birkmayer W, Horsey Kiewic O. «Der L-Dioxyphenolalalin (L-Dopa) Effekt bei der Parkinson-Akinese». Wien: Klein. Wochenschr. 1961; 73: 787-788.

Birkmayer W, Birkmayer JGD, Vrecko C. Paletta B, Reschenhofer E, Ott. E, «Nicotinamide adenine dinucleotide (NADH) as education for Parkinson`s disease. Experience with 415 patients». New Trends in Clinical Neuropharmacology 4(1) 7-24, 1990.

Birkmayer JGD. «The New Therapeutic approach for improving dementia of the Alzheimer type.» Ann. Clin. Lab. Sci. 1996; 26: 1-9.

Birkmayer JGD, Birkmayer W. «The Co-Enzyme nicotinamide adenide dinucleotide (NADH) as biological antidepressive agent experience with 205 patients. » New Trends in Clinical Neuropharmacology 1991; 5: 75-86.

Birkmayer, JGD & Vank, op. cit., 16

Vrecko K, Birkmayer JGD, Krainz J. «Stimulation of dopamine biosynthesis in culture p12 pheochromocytoma cells by the Co-Enzyme nicotinamide adenine dinocleotide (NADH).» J. Neural. Transm. 1996; 103: 1187-1193.

Birkmayer JGD, Vrecko C, Volc D, Birkmayer W. «Nicotinamide adenine dinucleotide (NADH) a new therapeutic approach to Parkinson´s disease, comparison of oral and paternal application».Actal Neurol. Scand. 1993; 87 (suppl 146): 32-35.

Stocchi V, KolbN, Cucchiarini L, Segni M, Magnani M, Fornaini G. «Adenine and pyridine nucleotidis during rabbit reticulocyte maturation and cell ageing. » Mechanisms of Ageing and Developmant 1987.

"Developing the therapeutic effect of stabilized NADH is, in my opinion, more important to mankind than the discovery of antibiotics."

Sir John Eccles, Nobel Prize Laureate of Medicine, 1964

In which cases could NADH be helpful?

- Regulation of blood pressure and cholesterol level
- Parkinson's and Alzheimer's disease
- Depressive moods
- Decreasing mental capabilities, forgetfulness
- Chronic fatigue syndrome, burnout syndrome
- Lethargy, energy slump
- Physical or mental exhaustion
- Lack of concentration, hyperactivity, ADHD
- Insomnia, jetlag
- Menopause problems
- Ageing processes (NADH is an anti-ageing enzyme)
- Reduced sexual activity in men and women
- Illnesses caused by free radicals, e. g. rheumatism, arthrosis etc.; NADH is one of the strongest anti-oxidants
- Illnesses caused by DNA damage, e.g. cancer, etc.; NADH might repair damaged cells
- Weakness of the immune system and all illnesses connected with it
  Obesity due to excessive eating; NADH has an appetite suppressing effect

Kornelia Sinning Health Care Products

Increased physical and mental performance with the important co-enzyme 1

NADH is a natural product and is suitable for people with allergies!

WITHOUT yeast, wheat, corn

WITHOUT lactose

WITHOUT sugar or artificial sweeteners

No intolerance or allergic reaction proven

No negative interactions with other drugs found

NADH is a natural product made from the living cells of brewer's yeast

For 10 mg of NADH, 20 kg of brewer's yeast are necessary

<u>Ask for your fax order sheet today at:</u>

Kornelia.Sinning@t-online.de

<u>Or order here:</u>

https://original-provence-lavendelhonig.versacommerce.de

Kornelia Sinning Health Care Products

Max-Hufschmidt-Str. 4, 55130 Mainz, Germany

Phone: ++49-3212-88 592 88 (electronic voicemail)

Your Questions and notebook